HUME IN 90 MINUTES

Hume
IN 90 MINUTES

Paul Strathern

IVAN R. DEE
CHICAGO

Library of Congress Cataloging-in-Publication Data:
Strathern, Paul, 1940–
    Hume in 90 minutes / Paul Strathern
      p.   cm. — (Philosophers in 90 minutes)
    Includes bibliographical references and index.
    ISBN 1-56663-239-0 (alk. paper). — ISBN 1-56663-240-4
(pbk. : alk. paper)
    1. Hume, David, 1711–1776.   I. Title.   II. Series.
B1498.S835   1999
192—dc21
  [b]   98-50207

Contents

HUME IN 90 MINUTES

Introduction

Before Hume, philosophers were often accused of being atheists. Hume was the first one who admitted it.

Being judged an atheist was not an enviable accolade for philosophers, or anyone else. Society had a way of dealing with such unorthodox thinkers—from ancient Greece (poison) to the Middle Ages (the Inquisition). Philosophers thus went to great lengths to convince everybody (and themselves) that they were not atheists. Hume's admission of theological bankruptcy was treated as a public scandal—but attempts to dissuade him were made with philosophical argument rather than the rack. This says as much for the tolerance of eighteenth-century British society as it does for Hume. Yet if he wished to remain consistent with his philosophy, Hume could have taken no other stance.

Philosophy was a long time coming to this. Several philosophers of the ancient world—such as some Stoics and a few cynics—were close to it. But Socrates was sentenced to death for not respecting the gods, and in ancient Rome it was often impossible not to believe in a god (especially when he was also the emperor). Thus faith became essential—for those who wished to continue thinking, just as much for those who wished to continue at all.

Early in the Christian era, philosophy was swallowed whole by theology. Plato and Aristotle became the holy writ, and philosophy consisted largely of elaborations on such accepted texts. These were followed by elaborations on the elaborations, and much heroic work rendering these elaborations acceptable to Christian dogma. A sideline developed with the misuse of logic in trying to prove the existence of God. A certain amount of all this activity was extremely ingenious, and even creative. But it was not original. The basic assumptions were always the same.

These assumptions were first seriously questioned in the seventeenth century by Descartes, who is now regarded as the founder of modern philosophy. Descartes swept aside the old assumptions and based his philosophy upon reason rather than faith. By a process of rational doubt, he showed that it is possible to deny everything—with one exception. I cannot doubt everything and yet at the same time doubt that I am thinking. "I think, therefore I am," was his celebrated conclusion. Thus Descartes reached the bedrock upon which he built the rational structure of his philosophy.

Just half a century later, the British philosopher John Locke went one step further with the introduction of empiricism. This claimed the ultimate ground of philosophy lay not in reason but in experience. In Locke's view, all that we know is gained ultimately from experience. We have no innate ideas—just sensations, and the ideas we gain from reflecting on these sensations. It looked as if philosophy had reached its limit.

But it wasn't long before someone took this one step further. The British empirical tradition took a step over the edge of sanity with the arrival of the Irishman Berkeley. If our knowledge of the world is based only on experience, how can we know that the world exists when we're not perceiving it? The world was thus reduced to a figment, and philosophy to a laughingstock. But fortunately for the world, Berkeley was a bishop and a God-fearing man. Of course the world continued to exist, he declared, even when no one was perceiving it. How could this be? Because the world was always being perceived by God.

This philosophical sleight of hand saved Berkeley a lot of trouble (and not only with his archbishop and his congregation). The world now had a prop. This was to last just thirty years, until Hume entered the fray.

Hume's Life and Works

Hume is the only philosopher whose ideas remain plausible to us today. The ancient Greeks are readable as high literature, but their philosophy seems like brilliant fairy tales. The medievalism of Augustine and Aquinas is alien to the modern sensibility. Descartes and the rationalists make us realize that the human condition is not rational; the earlier empiricists seem self-evident, wrongheaded, or absurd. And the philosophers after Hume fall mostly into either of the last two categories.

What I have just tried to do, Hume succeeded in doing—he reduced philosophy to ruins. Hume went one step further even than Berkeley and thought the empirical situation through to its logical conclusion. He denied the existence of everything—except our actual perceptions themselves. In doing this, he placed us in a difficult position. This is solipsism: I alone exist, and the world is nothing more than part of my consciousness. Here we arrive at the endgame of philosophy, one from which it's impossible to escape. Checkmate.

Then suddenly we realize that this doesn't matter. Regardless of what the philosophers say, the world remains there—we go on as before. As did Hume, whose gargantuan frame and ready wit were not that of a bewildered, Beckett-like solipsist thinking himself to bits. What Hume expressed was the *status* of our knowledge about the world. Neither the world of religion nor the world of science are certain. We can choose to believe in religion if we wish, but we do so on no certain evidence. And we can choose to make scientific deductions in order to impose our will upon the world. But neither religion nor science exist in themselves. They are merely our reactions to experience, one of any number of possible reactions.

Hume was descended from an auld Scots family. His biography by E. C. Mossner includes a family tree tracing his ancestors back to the Home of Home, who died in 1424. The philosopher's later ancestors include a number of unappealing but apparently distinguished Scottish names, such as a Belcher of Tofts, a Home of Blackadder, and a Norvell of Boghall.

David Hume was born April 24, 1711, in Edinburgh. His father died when he was three. A remarkably high proportion of the major philosophers lost their father at an early age, and this has produced the usual psychoanalytical theories. The gist of these is that the lack of a male parental figure creates a profound need for certainty. This in turn causes the bereft son to create an abstract system that takes the place of the "abstracted" parent. Such psychoanalytical theories can be brilliant, entertaining, and possibly even informative (though about what, I'm not quite sure). In other words, their resemblance to the philosophers they describe is uncanny in many aspects—except that of intellectual rigor.

By the time David Hume arrived on the scene, his branch of the distinguished family tree had descended to the point where it was living on the chilly little estate of Ninewells. This was nine miles west of Berwick-upon-Tweed, near the village of Chirnside on the Scottish border. The original house where the philosopher grew up no longer exists, but the gullible philosophic tourist is shown the "Philosopher's cave," down the slope to the southeast of the present house. This dank, cramped, uninviting aperture is where Hume is said to have meditated as a lad, as well as during his later years (when its inner reaches might have proved something of a tight fit for his ample form). If our thought is affected by our surroundings, we would expect Hume's meditations in this instance to have produced a somewhat neolithic philosophy with claustrophobic tendencies—and indeed this is much how the great German philosophers who came after him were to regard Hume's work. This was inevitable, as the Germans were intent upon constructing vast philosophical systems—baroque palaces of metaphysics, no less—and had no wish to occupy the primitive philosophic cave that Hume had bequeathed them. Alas, philosophy should not be confused with architectural aspiration.

Hume was brought up by his uncle, the local parish minister, who had succeeded the philosopher's father as the laird of Ninewells. Conditions at Ninewells would have appeared austere and primitive by modern standards: barefoot servants; the lower floor of the building containing the winter cowsheds and chicken runs; a diet based heavily on oatmeal, porridge, and kale (a nourishing traditional broth, or a disgusting watery cabbage soup, depending upon your taste). But Hume didn't feel that his childhood was deprived, either at the time or later. He was educated in the local schoolmaster's cottage with neighboring village children, in the egalitarian Scottish tradition that for so long surpassed its counterpart south of the border. Then, from the age of twelve to fifteen, he went to Edinburgh University. (Such early entry to Edinburgh University was quite normal at the time, a tradition that is maintained to this day in the demeanor of its students.)

After this, Hume was expected to study law. But he was already inclined otherwise and began reading voraciously over a wide range of subjects. Only with extreme reluctance did he devote any time at all to studying for the bar. This conflict continued for the next three years. Gradually Hume's reading began to concentrate more and more upon philosophy, until one day "there seem'd to be open'd up to me a New Scene of Thought." His philosophical ideas were beginning to crystallize, and he conceived the idea of writing down a system. By now the law "appear'd nauseous to me," and eventually he decided to give it up altogether.

This was no easy decision. It meant he was abandoning the chance of earning a professional living. The long inner struggle over this decision cost Hume dearly, and shortly afterward he had a nervous breakdown.

Hume went back to Ninewells, but his recovery was only intermittent. Between bouts of depression he continued excitedly pursuing his new ideas. The local physician was called in several times and was of the opinion that Hume was suffering from "the Disease of the Learned." He prescribed "a Course of Bitters & Anti-hysteric pills." He also advised Hume to take "an English Pint of Claret every day" and regular exercise in the form of long horseback rides.

Until now Hume had been tall and thin: a gawky fellow with gangling limbs. Yet despite his regimen of exercise, he now began putting on weight. On his daily rides into the bare, hilly countryside the horse became thinner as its rider expanded—gradually becoming the portly figure he was to remain for the rest of his life. This suggests that Hume's troubles during this period may in part have been glandular.

Hume's recovery was only gradual and may in fact never have been complete. Certain mysterious episodes during his later life suggest recurrent mental instability.

Hume had no wish to continue living with his mother at Ninewells forever. In 1734 a friend of the family found him a job as a clerk to a shipping merchant in Bristol. His motives for taking this job were various. He certainly needed the money. He also understood that the job would involve foreign travel. This appealed to his sense of adventure, and he also felt it would be beneficial for his mental health.

There is strong evidence that this continued to worry him. On his way to Bristol, Hume passed through London. Here he composed a long letter to Dr. Arbuthnott, one of the leading physicians of the day. In it, Hume does his best to describe his illness, though this description is severely hampered by the limited knowledge and inadequate concepts of the day. He describes his disease as "this Distemper," and refers to his "inflam'd Imaginations." He says: "I was continually fortifying myself with Reflections against Death, & Poverty, & Shame, & Pain, & all the other Calamities of Life." After outlining the remedies prescribed by his physician, he passes inconsequentially to some philosophical reflections: "I believe 'tis a certain fact that most of the Philosophers who have gone before us, have been overthrown by the greatness of their genius, & that little more is requir'd to make a man succeed in this Study than to throw off all Prejudices either for his own Opinions or for this of others." Hume ends by asking various questions about his illness ("Whether I can hope for a Recovery?"), which he answers himself ("Assuredly you can"). And this appears to have done the trick. Hume never sent his ten-page letter (though he kept it all his life). He seems to have found that the mere writing of it was a cure in itself. Or at least as near a cure as he would ever find.

Hume now settled down to work in Bristol and discovered that his job as a clerk was unlikely to involve any foreign travel. Relations with his employer gradually deteriorated, and eventually he left his job. By his twenty-fourth birthday he was back at Ninewells, where he began to get a bad name for his "superior and irreligious ways." By this stage Hume had inherited a small private income of forty pounds sterling a year, which enabled him to live frugally without having to work.

He now set about writing down his philosophical observations, with the aim of creating a new philosophy which would make him famous. (Throughout his life Hume made little secret of his ultimate aim: "my love of literary fame, my ruling passion." And it was as a literary figure, more than as a philosopher, that Hume was to achieve fame. In later life Boswell was to refer to him as "the greatest writer in Britain," and to this day he is listed in the British Library catalog as "David Hume, the historian.") After a few months Hume decided to set off for France. Here he could live well on his small private income, and in isolation he would be able to concentrate on his new philosophy without interruption or speculations of a more practical nature. (At Ninewells there was always mother and his uncle, neither of whom were philosophy fans.)

There is a story that Hume left Ninewells in a hurry. Not long after he went to France an unmarried young local woman called Agnes, who was said to have "a bad record with such matters," announced that she was pregnant. The attitude toward this kind of thing in Scotland at the time was all very Christian. Poor deserted

Agnes was exhibited at church, where the parish minister (Hume's uncle) delivered the customary public denouncement, which ended with the pious hope that she would die in childbirth. As if this display of compassion and Christian love were not enough, Agnes was then hauled before the sessions, where she almost certainly received a further punishment—again, probably involving some kind of public humiliation, always a favored method of retribution in a hypocritical society. (I'm told that this is due to unconscious masochism: the thrill induced by the fact that *you* haven't yet been caught.) During the course of Agnes's examination at the session, she eventually named the absent Hume as the father of her unborn child—probably to protect the real father. This was the sessions' firm conviction, at any rate. We will never know the truth.

With one notable exception, this is the main evidence we have of Hume's sexual inclinations. According to Mossner, Hume "in later life, in Italy and France and Scotland, was to prove a man of normal sexual desires." Since not much else is recorded about these sexual desires, one can only assume they were fulfilled by hospitality—with enthusiastic chambermaids and demanding hostesses. And since Hume is one of the few literary figures of the age who didn't catch the pox, it's unlikely that this hospitality was very frequent, or that he went with whores, who at the time were cheaper than hot water bottles. (This latter is intended as a purely socioeconomic observation, with no sexist undertones. These disease-ridden human hot water bottles would in most cases have arrived at their condition after suffering the same fate as Agnes, victims of the hypocrisy so necessary to any upright society of closet masochists.)

Hume went first to live in Reims but later moved to La Fleche, almost certainly because of its inspiring associations with Descartes, who had been educated there at the Jesuit college. Within three years Hume had finished *A Treatise of Human Nature*. He was later to disparage this work because of what he considered to be its youthful extravagances. But he did not disavow its philosophy, which contains almost all the original philosophical ideas for which he is today remembered. Bertrand Russell, in his *History of Western Philosophy*, is even of the view that this work contains the best parts of Hume's philosophy. Some achievement for a man who was not yet thirty.

In *A Treatise of Human Nature* Hume attempted to define the basic principles of human knowledge. How do we know anything for certain? And what exactly is it that we do know for certain? In trying to answer these questions he followed in the empiricist tradition, believing that all our knowledge is ultimately based on experience. In Hume's view, experience consists of perceptions, of which there are two types. "Those perceptions which enter with most force and violence we may name *impressions*; and, under this name, I comprehend all our sensations, passions and emotions, as they make their first appearance in the soul. By *ideas* I mean the faint images of these in thinking and reasoning."

He explains: "Every simple idea has a simple impression, which resembles it." But we can also form complex ideas. These are derived from impressions, by way of simple ideas, but need

23

not necessarily conform to an impression. For example, we can imagine a mermaid by combining our idea of a fish and our idea of a woman.

By adhering strictly to this notion of impressions and ideas as the only certain basis for our knowledge, Hume arrives at some astonishing conclusions. Objects, continuity, the self, even cause and effect—all these are shown to be fallacious notions. We never actually experience an object—only impressions of its color, shape, consistency, taste, and so forth. Likewise we have no actual impression that corresponds to continuity. Things simply happen one after another. We can't even say that one thing causes another to happen. We may observe one thing constantly following another (lit gunpowder, explosion), but there is no logical connection between the two, and no logical reason why they will happen in sequence in the future. "We have no other notion of cause and effect, but that of certain objects which have been *always conjoined* together." Induction, by a process of simple enumeration, has no logical force. All swans had been white before the discovery in Hume's time of black swans in Australia. Thus swans had not been necessarily white, any more than a flame necessarily caused gunpowder to explode.

There are many difficulties in Hume's approach, and these are not just limited to common sense. How can we possibly carry on living if this is all we know for certain? Hume was well aware of this objection to his philosophy. "When we leave our closet, and engage in the common affairs of life, its conclusions seem to vanish, like the phantoms of the night on the appearance of morning; and it is difficult for us to retain even that conviction, which we had attain'd with difficulty." What in fact Hume was pointing out was the utter precariousness of the human condition with regard to knowledge. We *think* we know a great deal—but in reality much of what we think we know is mere supposition. Reliable supposition, but supposition nonetheless.

This position is strangely similar to the state of knowledge today, when the ultimate truths of science have long since departed the realms of credibility or common sense. We grudgingly accept the truths of science, which would have us believe that a torrent of subatomic particles streams through our solid earth, shadows of anti-matter dog our every step, and a curve ball of space would carry us into the past. Yet we continue to live our lives in a Newtonian universe, with ripe apples falling by gravity onto the cozy lawns of reality. Today the high ground of what we are assured is the truth is no less nonsensical than in Hume's philosophy. And, as ever, the laughably inadequate notions of common sense continue to suffice.

Despite Hume's destruction of the basis for all science, he had the highest regard for Newton and his experimental approach. Indeed, Hume's notion of impressions may well have been inspired by a passage from Newton's *Optics* about light rays and objects: "In them there is nothing else than a certain power and disposition to stir up a sensation of this or that color." (In other words, we don't experience the object itself.) Hume had the deepest admiration for science, especially for the rigor of its methods. He felt sure this was the way to a better future. Yet paradoxically, Hume's philosophy plunges humanity back into the past, to a position that it hadn't occupied since the Middle Ages. Copernicus had displaced humanity and the earth from the center of the universe. Hume's solipsist empiricism firmly reestablished humanity at the center of whatever was going on (though in Hume's case this didn't actually include the earth, let alone the universe).

Hume's position has many interesting anomalies. Berkeley had relied upon God to prop up the world when we weren't looking. With Hume, there was no world to prop up. And if there are no such things as corporeal bodies, continuity, or cause and effect, there is scarcely room for a God. Hume may not have believed in God, but his philosophy reduces us to a situation remarkably close to that of certain Buddhist mystics (who also don't believe in God). Where Berkeley had reduced philosophy to a joke, Hume explained the joke (away). But this was unlikely to induce people to take it any more seriously.

In 1739 Hume returned to Britain and published his *Treatise*. He then sat back, waiting for the savage and vitriolic attacks that would inevitably appear from the critics—to which he would reply with consummate brilliance, thus guaranteeing him fame, money, public notoriety, the widespread approbation of poets and financiers, the love of fair women and financiers' wives, and all the other little marks of recognition that any tyro philosopher comes to expect as his due. Alas, this was not to be. Hume's great masterpiece "fell deadborn from the press," as he put it. His work suffered the worst fate of all: no one noticed. And Hume's reaction? "Being naturally of a cheerful and sanguine temper, I very soon recovered from the blow." He returned to Edinburgh and began writing essays on moral and political topics. These achieved some recognition, and in 1744 he put himself forward as candidate for the Chair of Moral Philosophy at Edinburgh University. Unfortunately it appeared that at least one person had after all read his *Treatise of Human Nature*. A vehement objection was lodged against Hume's candidature, citing his *Treatise* and claiming that it was

a work of heresy and atheism. These were difficult charges to deny, especially to someone who
had evidently read the book. (Hume's earlier in-
tention to dazzle the outraged critics with his
brilliant ripostes had presumably been based on
the assumption that these critics wouldn't take
the unprecedented step of actually reading his
work.) Hume wasn't given the job at his old university, and he left Edinburgh in disgust.

Hume now decided to look for a job more
suited to his abilities. Eventually he was offered
the post of tutor to the mad Marquess of Anan-
dale at his home near St. Albans in Southeast England. This appeared to fit the bill, and Hume
accepted. During the periods when his lordship
was beyond even philosophic instruction (which
appears to have been considered as a last resort),
Hume started to write a history of England, but
he soon became so dispirited that he gave up,
promising himself that he would return to this
project later.

The country too was now in the grip of its
own insanity—namely, the 1745 Jacobite Rebellion against English rule in Scotland. A Scottish

army of five thousand men successfully invaded England, then retreated in embarrassment, and were finally massacred at the Battle of Culloden. Fortunately for Hume he was in England throughout the rebellion and was thus able to observe it with some detachment. A number of his friends in Edinburgh were forced to take sides, with unfortunate consequences. Hume's dry comment on the affair was, "Eight millions of people [might] have been subdued and reduced to slavery by five thousand, the bravest, but still the most worthless amongst them."

This episode had a profound effect on Hume. He had seen history unfolding around him, even if he hadn't been directly involved in it. This deficiency was soon remedied when he was sacked from the job of tutoring a lunatic and forced to lower his sights still further by becoming secretary to a general.

General James St. Clair was waiting to set off on a military expedition against the French in Canada when he took on his new secretary. The ships and the army for this expedition had all been assembled at Portsmouth for several months. But the secretary of state, the Duke of Newcastle, couldn't make up his mind about precisely what to do with them. This was the man of whom it was said that he lost half an hour every morning, and spent the rest of the day looking for it. Against some very stiff competition indeed, this period is frequently judged as the most incompetent in British military history: ideal subject matter for our budding philosophical historian, who was now on hand to witness for himself the awesome wonder of the military mind at work.

The Duke of Newcastle finally found his lost half-hour and ordered General St. Clair's expedition to put to sea and attack the French—not in Canada, but in France. When General St. Clair asked the duke what they were expected to do with the specially selected and trained Indian trackers they had on board, this question was dismissed as irrelevant. The general then asked *where* in France he was expected to launch his attack, and was told that anywhere would do. General St. Clair (together with his new secretary) caught the stagecoach back to Portsmouth and went on board the expedition's flagship. Here he discovered a problem. No one on any of the ships had a map of France. Hume advanced the information that he knew what it looked like, and could even draw a sketch if the general wished. But in the end an officer was sent ashore to see if anything could be found in the local bookshop. He came back with a secondhand book about France, which happened to have a small map in the back. Hume confirmed that it was definitely the right shape, and the general set sail for France—having been informed that he couldn't miss it as long as he sailed due south.

The British fleet finally arrived off L'Orient (whose position on the southwest coast of Brittany, that is, not facing Britain, suggests that General St. Clair may initially have succeeded in missing France). Just along the coast from L'Orient the general landed his army (while Hume avidly took notes for his projected history of England). The general's aim was to besiege the important naval harbor at L'Orient, but unfortunately soon after he landed it began to rain. His three thousand troops had been cooped up on board their ships for months and began suffering from cramps as they marched through the mud. In the end they couldn't even stand upright. (Common sense suggests that something a little stronger than rainwater may have contributed to this condition.) Meanwhile, inside L'Orient the French discovered they outnumbered the British invasion force by seven to one. The two opposing forces exchanged a few rounds of cannon fire, and the military geniuses on either side then retired to ponder the situation over dinner. The British high command soon came to the conclusion that their legless troops were better off on board ship, and marched them back under cover of darkness. Meanwhile the French commander, for reasons that only an expert military mind could possibly fathom, had decided to surrender. When the large French force arrived to surrender next morning, they discovered a few disconsolate British artillery men whom everyone seemed to have forgotten about, sheltering from the rain beside their dripping guns. The French now found themselves with a superiority of nearly five thousand to one. Wisely realizing that the sheer logistics of having to accept the surrender of so many men was obviously beyond these few ridiculous Britishers, the French changed their tactics and took the Britishers prisoner. Meanwhile the British fleet and its philosopher-in-residence got lost in a storm, and after various adventures they all sailed home to collect their medals.

As a result of this glorious campaign, General St. Clair was rewarded with the leadership of an important diplomatic mission to Vienna and Turin. He set off, accompanied by his secretary and staff of diplomatic advisers.

Hume reacted variously to his travels through Europe. "Germany is . . . full of industrious honest People, & were it united it would be the greatest Power that ever was in the world," he noted perceptively. "The common People are here, almost every where, much better treated & more at their Ease, than in France; and not very much inferior to the English, notwithstanding all the Airs the latter give themselves." But Hume wasn't quite so impressed by the Austrians in

Styria: "as much as the Country is agreeable in its Wildness; as much are the Inhabitants savage & deform'd & monstrous in their Appearance. Very many of them have ugly swelld Throats: Idiots and Deaf People swarm in every Village; and the general Aspect of the People is the most shocking I ever saw. One wou'd think, that as this was the great Road, thro which all the barbarous Nations made their Irruptions into the Roman Empire, they always left here the Refuse of their Armies before they entered into the Enemies Country." Hume's reaction was not just an attack of spleen occasioned by the tiresome and enervating rigors of stagecoach travel through the Alps. His observations were no exaggeration, even if his diagnosis was wide of the mark. It's now known that this region suffered from an iodine deficiency in the diet, resulting in widespread goiter and lunacy.

But the locals weren't the only ones to suffer from mental derangement. When the mission reached Turin, Hume fell ill. A fellow member of the mission recorded: "He was affected by a most violent Fever, attended with its natural

Symptoms, Delerium and Ravings. In the Parox-
isms of his Disorder he often talked, with much
seeming Perturbation, of the Devil, of Hell, and
of Damnation, and one night, while his Nurse-
tender happened to be asleep, He rose from his
Bed, and made towards a deep Well, which was
in the Court-yard, with a Design, as was sup-
posed, to drown himself, but, finding the Back
Door Locked, He rushed into a room where,
upon a Couch, the Gentlemen of the Family
were, He well knew, used to deposit their
Swords, and here he was found by the Servants
who had been awakened by the noise He had
made at the door in endeavouring to open it, and
was by them forcibly brought back to his Bed."

Hume appears to have quickly recovered,
and this "whimsical Adventure" became a source
of merriment amongst the company. Hume took
a more sober view of it, remonstrating: "Do
you suppose Philosophy to be proof against
Madness? The Organisation of my Brain was
impaired, and I was as mad as any Man in Bed-
lam." Hume appears to have been fully aware
of, and feared, his largely latent mental disorder.

And we can only speculate about its possible effect on his intellectual activities—though it's intriguing that such a thoroughgoing atheist should reveal manic fears of the devil, hell, and damnation. Likewise, one can only wonder how many other similar episodes occurred that were not recorded. Many important questions here will probably never be answered.

General St. Clair and his secretary eventually brought their mission to a successful conclusion, having traveled all through Europe and achieved nothing. (It's the achievements in this field that usually spell disaster.) Hume then decided he'd had enough. Having educated a madman and served as secretary to a general, he now felt himself suitably qualified to reenter the philosophic fray. He returned to Edinburgh, where he set about rewriting his great philosophic flop. The first part he turned into *An Enquiry Concerning Human Understanding*, the work that was to spread his ideas throughout Europe. The last part he turned into *An Enquiry Concerning the Principles of Morals*, which he always mistakenly believed to be his finest work.

It may be difficult for some to see how a philosophical solipsist, who had exploded the notion of cause and effect, continuity, and even bodies, could embark upon a moral philosophy. But where ethics is concerned, Hume chooses to ignore the conclusions of his thoroughgoing empiricism in the *Enquiry*. He does, however, attempt to relate his ethics to the structure of his empiricism. Thus passions observed in others are received as impressions. Compassion, on the other hand, begins as an idea, but if it is sufficiently strong and lively can become an impression. As one would expect from Hume's temperament, his moral philosophy is essentially humane. Compassion, or sympathy, is seen as the basis of all moral qualities. This brings personal happiness as well as social benefit. Hume esteems moral qualities according to their usefulness or their agreeableness—with regard to the individual and the community. These ideas had developed from the democratic liberalism of Locke, which placed emphasis on a social contract guaranteeing citizens natural rights under the law. Hume's ideas were to have a formative influence on the nineteenth-century Utilitarians, such as Bentham and Mill, who developed them into the formula "the greatest happiness of the greatest number." But this laudable wish for social happiness had an inherent flaw. What of the scapegoat whose public hanging will give so much joy to the majority of the populace? Reducing public morality to a mathematical equation, with the majority carrying the day on all matters, leaves minorities vulnerable to discrimination.

In 1752 Hume was made keeper of the Advocates' Library in Edinburgh. This far from onerous employment gave him the opportunity to write more philosophical essays on a wide variety of subjects. The essay was all the rage at the time as the latest fashionable literary form. Although Hume was not as stylistically brilliant as Addison and Steele, his ideas were more profound. The topics of his essays ranged from disparate subjects such as politics and standards of public taste, through analogous topics such as tragedy and marriage, to subjects as similar as polygamy and stoicism. His essays on economic topics included many formative ideas in this embryonic pseudoscience. And his essays on miracles (no such thing) and suicide (up to you) were to cause a sensation when they were finally published.

As a result of his employment with General St. Clair, Hume had now seen firsthand what history was all about. Heartened by this insight he decided to embark once more upon his *History of England*. This begins with the invasion of Julius Caesar in 55 B.C. and ends with the Glorious Revolution of 1688. Hume finally finished his history in 1762, having progressed at the rate of a century a year, the same rate as Gibbon claimed while writing his *Decline and Fall of the Roman Empire*, which was published four years later. Hume's *History* was ranked as second only to Gibbon's masterpiece but consistently outsold it and remained a best-seller for almost a century (until Macaulay's *History* became the standard work).

Hume's *History of England* is highly readable and was one of the first to broaden its scope by including the cultural and scientific interests of the period. Because it refused to subscribe to contemporary prejudices, it was immediately labeled as hopelessly biased. Hume's cultural comments strike me as being quite fair. He spoke of the poets of the previous century producing "monuments of genius perverted by indecency and bad taste, but none more than Dryden . . . both by reason of the greatness of his talents and the gross abuse he made of them." And his philosophical views often obtrude to fine effect: "While Newton seemed to draw off the veil from some of the mysteries of nature, he showed at the same time the imperfections of the mechanised philosophy; and thereby restored her ultimate secrets to that obscurity, in which they ever did and ever will remain."

A year after Hume published his *History of England*, he was honored by having all his works placed on the Roman Catholic Index of banned books. In the centuries before our era, this accolade was very similar to the Nobel Prize. It concentrated on genuine scientific, humanitarian, and literary achievements but was occasionally extended to charlatans or harmless mediocrities for political reasons.

In 1763 Hume was appointed secretary to the British ambassador in France. (The war so successfully waged by the likes of General St. Clair and the commander of the garrison at L'Orient had eventually been called to a halt by the forces of sanity.) Hume's appointment in Paris was a huge success. He was now regarded as the British Voltaire and was lionized by fashionable society. The ambassador quickly realized that his secretary's presence on the salon circuit was worth far more to promote British interests than anything else the embassy could offer, and encouraged him to attend as many parties as possible.

By now Hume was a repulsive figure. He was bloated and red in the face, ate too much, enjoyed his drink, and was generally rather clumsy. But he was also highly intelligent and had a fine droll wit. The French had never seen anything like this before. To them, elegance and wit were virtually synonymous. For one to appear without a semblance of the other was a truly British eccentricity. Owing to Hume's extreme ungainliness, he was even excused from bowing at court, and after one hilarious disaster was also no longer required to make his exit walking backward toward the door. Hume was presented to the king and all the members of his family— even his young grandchildren, who each had to memorize a little speech in honor of "M'sieur Yoome" and how they were looking forward to reading his *History of England*.

Despite Hume's appearance and enjoyment of social occasions, he was not exactly a happy man. Inwardly he kept a tight rein on his emotions. He enjoyed the company of women but privately characterized himself as "a gallant who gives no offence to husbands and lovers." Yet all this lionizing caused him momentarily to drop his guard. When he encountered a beautiful and intelligent woman, who indicated that she was interested in him physically, he quickly fell for her.

But this was France, where such things are never simple. The Comtesse de Boufflers was the mistress of the Prince de Conti, one of the most powerful political figures in the land. She was thirty-eight, Hume was fifty-two. They quickly became friends but were both wary of further involvement. They corresponded, using the elaborate manners of the period as a subtle, devious and often flimsy disguise for their true emotions. Hume told her: "You have saved me from a total indifference towards every thing in human life." But in the end it seems they were both afraid of each other, and each became convinced of the futility of the situation. Nothing came of it, and when Hume returned to England in 1765 they never met again. Yet they did continue to correspond, and the last letter we have in Hume's hand is addressed to his understanding countess.

It was the Comtesse de Boufflers who was instrumental in Hume's meeting Rousseau, the great French political theorist and philosopher. Nowadays it's customary to characterize Rousseau as a madman and a bastard (in the pejorative sense), whose ideas lead directly to social evil of the worst kind. And there's no denying this case. Rousseau was mentally unsta-

44

ble; he personally delivered, one by one, all five of his infant children by his mistress to the foundlings' home down the street; and his ideas do encourage unprincipled behavior. He believed that true virtue lay in the "noble savage" who was uncorrupted by civilization. He was against a social contract that guaranteed natural rights and in favor of dictate by the "general will." This he felt was bound to be directed toward the common good, and when the individual voluntarily subjected himself to it, he would be "forced to be free." Inevitably this has an ominous ring to twentieth-century ears. Rousseau's ideas were to inspire both the glories and the excesses of the French Revolution, and continued to play a similar role in the twentieth century. His ideas are recognizable in fascism and communism as well as in the underlying drift toward self-expression and liberalism.

But the Rousseau who met Hume was more than just a time bomb of explosive ideas. As a man he is best understood as the genius who inspired the romantic movement, and personally as a walking naked sensibility. He was the precise opposite of Hume, both temperamentally and philosophically. And yet they were both on the same side. They both strove for reform. The old Europe of absolute monarchs and the landed gentry was beginning to give way to a more communal urban society, with liberal democratic tendencies. A process of evolution had started with Descartes and progressed with the rise of the introspective novel. Europe was witnessing the advent of a widespread self-consciousness: the birth of an individuality that thought for itself. Rousseau's concern was with individuality itself, its expression and self-realization. Hume was concerned with the condition of thinking for oneself and seeing the world through eyes cleansed of the old preconceptions. There is no such thing as a soul, no one has ever perceived a "mind," we experience no causality or God. Rousseau, on the other hand, produced no coherent philosophy but will be remembered forever for resonant ideas such as "the noble savage" and sayings such as "Man was born free, but everywhere he is in chains."

Rousseau was on the run (after publishing

Émile, which supported democracy and denied the divine right of kings), and Hume offered to look after him. Unfortunately, by the time Rousseau arrived in England he had been driven insane by his persecutors. He would embrace Hume, saying how much he loved him; but within no time he would become convinced that Hume was in league with his enemies and plotting against him. Hume did his best, Rousseau did his worst. To everyone's relief, Rousseau eventually fled to France—where he began spreading all kinds of slanders against Hume. The philosopher had met the genius, and neither had understood the other. The nature of their meeting was ominously symbolic—the struggle between their two positions continues to this day.

In 1769 Hume returned to live in Edinburgh. By now he was enormous—"the fattest of Epicurus's hogs," according to Gibbon (who was no lightweight himself: his comment on Hume was intended as approbation). Hume continued to work hard, revising and rewriting his *History* and his philosophical works, and writing essays.

He also wrote an oddly objective and evasive autobiography. Perhaps he didn't wish to give ammunition to his enemies, who were many. To the conservative elements of the establishment—the church, orthodox academia, etc.—he remained anathema. On the other hand, an anonymous pamphlet called "Character of—by himself," which was certainly about Hume and almost certainly by him, contains deep insights into his character and self-assessment. "A very good man the constant purpose of whose life is to do mischief." "An enthusiast without religion, a philosopher who despairs to attain the truth." "Exempt from vulgar prejudices, full of his own."

Hume now became the famous old man of Edinburgh. He enjoyed dining at length with his friends, who became known as the "Eaterati." But he also continued to discuss his ideas with his intellectual peers, such as his longtime friend Adam Smith, the social philosopher and pioneering theoretical economist. Hume and Smith shared many ideas on social philosophy, and it has been suggested that Hume even influenced

Smith in his theory that the interests of society are best guided by the "invisible hand" of competition. This hand, which shaped the twentieth century, looks set to throttle the twenty-first when there will be strictly limited resources for which to compete—but neither Hume nor Smith should be held responsible for the blindness of present-day economists. They lived at the dawning of an era of seemingly unlimited possibilities (in so many spheres), an era on which the sun is now fast setting.

But in other respects Hume's ideas are often in deep accord with those of the twentieth century. "If we take in our hand any volume—of divinity or school metaphysics, for instance—let us ask: 'Does it contain any abstract reasoning concerning quantity or number?' No. 'Does it contain any experimental reasoning concerning matter of fact and existence?' No. Commit it then to the flames, for it can contain nothing but sophistry and illusion." And: "The whole world presents nothing but the idea of a blind Nature . . . pouring forth from her lap, without discernment or parental care, her maimed and abortive children." Such opinions were a rarity in the mid-eighteenth century.

Gradually Hume's physique and lifestyle began to take their toll. He became increasingly ill, and eventually two eminent surgeons were called in to examine him. One after the other they prodded their fingers and squeezed his massive stomach; in the end they agreed that he was suffering from a tumor of the liver. Ever the bold but skeptical seeker after truth, Hume prodded his own fingers into his stomach and personally confirmed their diagnosis, discovering a tumor "about the Bigness of an Egg," which was "flat and round."

His health gradually failed, and he lost a lot of weight. Word got around that Hume was dying, and people flocked from far and wide to see if the great atheist would repent on his deathbed. Boswell arrived to find that Hume was "lean, ghastly and quite of an earthy appearance." (It's difficult to decide whether this last observation is inexact or profound.) But when Boswell asked Hume if he believed it was possible there was an afterlife, "He answered, It was possible a piece of coal put on the fire would not burn."

At the end of a long illness, Hume died on August 25, 1776 (without repenting). A considerable crowd gathered outside his door to watch the funeral procession of "the Atheist"; but he was not an unpopular figure with the mob, only the church. And unlike the great philosophers to come, his philosophy remains plausible. But there's one snag. When we read Hume's philosophy we recognize that we think like this—but we know that we don't live like this. Is it possible that this time philosophy was right, and that *we* are the ones who are wrong?

Afterword

Epistemology, the investigation of the grounds for knowledge, was seen by many as the core of philosophy. Before Hume, epistemology had been a thriving industry, producing all kinds of theories. Upon these were based the amazing systems that were the pride and joy of philosophy. This was philosophy's main selling point: a system that explained *everything*. With Hume, the bottom fell out of the market. Hume showed that the construction of philosophical systems was no longer possible. But it is in the nature of philosophy to attempt the impossible. In the era immediately following Hume, German philosophers were to produce the grandest philosophical systems known to man.

Kant read Hume and claimed that this experience "awoke me from my dogmatic slumbers." As a result, Kant produced an all-embracing system of the highest ingenuity and insight. This in turn was followed by Hegel, who produced the greatest philosophical dinosaur of them all—a metaphysical system so vast and complex as to be well beyond the comprehension of mere mortals. It was Nietzsche who saw that these misguided attempts could only produce extinct beasts. In Nietzsche's view, there "was more sense in a page of Hume than in the entire works of Hegel."

Yet even Nietzsche failed to clear the epistemological hurdle that Hume had placed in the way of philosophic advance—admitting that Hume's objections (to almost everything) were unanswerable. The only way to proceed was to ignore them. We had to continue to philosophize regardless—just as we continued to live regardless of Hume's demolition of continuity. There were always lots of other things to philosophize about.

In the twentieth century Wittgenstein adopted a comparable approach. Cavalierly ignoring Hume (to the point of not even bothering to read him), Wittgenstein soon arrived at a remarkably similar philosophic position. (Great minds don't always think alike because they plagiarize the same sources.)

Hume may well have pushed Humpty-Dumpty from the wall, but still nobody has worked out how to put him together again. Nowadays philosophy insists upon ignoring certain questions (which it deems unanswerable). It's worth noting that it also ignores certain answers.

Hume, His True Successors, and Modern Science

Hume's extreme brand of empiricism may have been destructive of philosophy and religion, but it was to clear the way for a brave new world. Here there would be no straitjacket of tradition, the old certainties could be questioned, nothing was sacred any more—except the truth, and this was available to everyone through experience. Implicit in Hume's philosophy was a belief in existential self-responsibility. From here it was but a short step to a belief in progress, democracy, and science—the shibboleths of our age.

Not for nothing was the first true successor

to Hume both a philosopher and a physicist. Ernst Mach was born in Austria in 1838 and grew up during the grand era of German metaphysical systems (Kant, Hegel, and Marx were regarded as the philosophers of the day). Ironically, Mach is most widely remembered today for one of his comparatively minor achievements: his work in supersonics. When an object reaches the speed of sound it breaks the "sound barrier": this takes place at Mach 1, which is named after him.

As a scientist, Mach had deep sympathy with Hume's empiricism and theory of knowledge. This was how science worked—or ought to work, in Mach's view. Unlike almost all other philosophers, Mach knew enough about science to begin applying Hume's ideas to some effect. By the second half of the nineteenth century, science was going through a transcendent phase similar to philosophy. It had grown too big for its boots and had an absurdly overblown view of its own powers—both to conquer the world and to explain it (a recurrent scientific malady, which once again reached fever pitch toward the end of the following century). Science believed it could know everything. The entire universe worked according to mechanical laws which could be discovered by science. Such laws of nature had an existence of their own which could not be questioned by mere philosophy.

Mach was to explode this overinflated balloon, and his arguments are recognizably Humean. The so-called laws of nature were nothing more than generalizations from innumerable particular experiences. Only such experiences existed; the generalizations were no more than man-made ideas with no independent existence of their own whatsoever.

Mach's development of Hume's ideas struck a jarring note in the great scientific era of Darwin, Faraday, and Mendeleyev. But Hume's ideas could well withstand such scientific giants, having been inspired by, and tempered by, the findings of Newton. Hume had a profound understanding of science, and his ideas remained relevant despite the previously unparalleled advances that science had made during the century between him and Mach.

When Mach began applying Hume's ideas, he soon found himself questioning some of the basic assumptions of nineteenth-century science. According to Mach, all you could say about space was the distribution and behavior of the phenomena within it. This was what related matter thoughout the universe, not the fact of it being in something called space—which couldn't be observed or even registered instrumentally, *by definition*. In other words, there was no such thing as absolute space: it was simply a concept. Likewise, time. No one had actually measured anything called time. It was only an idea. All we experienced, and could measure, was one set of movements (a runner, say) against another set of movements (the controlled, standardized movements of a stopwatch). Thus, no such things as absolute time either. (A few years later Einstein would acknowledge that Mach's idea of time had prompted his thinking about relativity.)

But this approach to epistemology contained the seeds of its own downfall (and as we shall see, possibly even the downfall of epistemology as a philosophic enterprise). Mach also applied his Humean ideas to the atom. By the latter half of the nineteenth century the concept of the atom was beginning to play a major role in both chemistry and physics. (Mendeleyev built his Periodic Table of the Elements on the idea of different types of atoms; Avogadro's revolutionary hypothesis about the similar density of gases relied upon the notion of the atom.) Yet no one had actually ever *seen* an atom (or measured one, or come up with any observational evidence whatsoever for the existence of such a thing). Science was moving beyond observation into the field of hypothesis based upon *what worked* as an explanation. Atoms worked as an explanation, and the notion of the atom was proving highly fruitful in further extending scientific knowledge. So what if the existence of atoms couldn't be proved—this didn't matter. Mach, and thus Hume, were wrong. Or so it would seem. Nowadays we are all convinced that there are such things as atoms. Or are we? What exactly are these things called atoms?

Atoms, as conceived by late-nineteenth-century scientists, were like miniscule indestructible billiard balls. Mach contradicted this notion, on Humean grounds, and he was right to do so. We now know that atoms are not miniscule indestructible billiard balls. According to modern science they are something much more complex and ambiguous. Indeed, by the early decades of the twentieth century quantum physicists had begun to question the whole idea of "picturing" the atom at all. According to the great German scientist Heisenberg (he of the famous Uncertainty Principle), it was not possible to describe such a thing as an atom. All we could do was take observations of what happened at this physical level, and record the data. Such data could be read only as a series of tables, and was not to be hung onto some "picture" of an atom. All such pictures were concepts, not based on any observation, which could only be misleading. Mach's approach (Hume's empiricism) appeared to have some relevance after all. (The resemblance between Heisenberg's tables of data, with no overall picture, and Hume's simple impressions, with no objects or causality, is uncanny.)

Mach's ideas were to have a profound influence on one of the major philosophical movements of the early twentieth century, namely, logical positivism. This was the product of a group of philosophers, scientists, and mathematicians who met regularly in the cafés of Vienna and became known as the Vienna Circle. The multidisciplinary nature of the group indicates the direction in which philosophy was now moving.

The core principles of logical positivism have an unmistakably Humean ring to them. According to these, there are two types of meaningful statements. The first contains the propositions of logic and pure mathematics. These are necessarily true because they are tautologous—that is, the meaning of one concept is contained in the concept to which it refers. (For example: $2 + 2 = 4$—the concept $2 + 2$ contains the concept of 4.) The second type of meaningful proposition contains facts which, unlike the previous type, refer to the empirical world. For example: "It is raining," "The speed of light is precisely 186,282 miles per second." We can verify these facts (or disprove them) by referring to experience, or we can test their validity by experiment. All propositions that did not fit into these two categories were deemed by the logical positivists to be metaphysical twaddle. Such propositions were neither necessary (in the logical sense) nor verifiable in any way. For example: "God created the universe," "Life has no meaning."

Unfortunately it was soon realized that the core principles of logical positivism also fell into this category. They were not logically necessary, nor could they be proved by experience. Despite this damning flaw, logical positivism proved a useful corrective to the inflated metaphysics of the nineteenth century. It attempted a scientific way of doing philosophy and proved of immense use to scientists during the 1920s and 1930s, when the likes of Einstein and Bohr were recreating our entire universe. But with the advent of relativity and quantum theory, science itself now seemed to be progressing in an unscientific fashion. Take quantum theory, for instance, which treats light as either particles or waves. This is basically illogical—a thing cannot be two separate things at once. But as a theory *it works*, and produces further fruitful knowledge. Here theory is built upon theory—with experience (or experimentally verifiable data) as the *end product*. In such a situation *any* philosophic theory of epistemology would seem inadequate. For the time being it appears that science has simply hijacked epistemology. Yet should epistemology ever return to the domain of philosophy, it will surely be on a Humean basis.

From Hume's Writings

The definition of impressions and ideas:
All the perceptions of the human mind resolve themselves into two distinct kinds, which I shall call IMPRESSIONS and IDEAS. The differences betwixt these consists in the degrees of force and liveliness, with which they strike our mind, and make their way into our thought or consciousness. Those perceptions, which enter with most force and violence, we may name *impressions*; and under this name I comprehend all our sensations, passions and emotions, as they make their first appearance in the soul. By *ideas* I mean the faint images of these in thinking and reasoning; such as, for instance, are all the perceptions ex-

cited by the present discourse, excepting only, those which arise from the sight and touch, and excepting the immediate pleasure or unease it may occasion.

—*A Treatise of Human Nature*, Book 1

Explaining our perceptions further:
There is another division of our perceptions, which it will be convenient to observe, and which extends itself both to our impressions and ideas. The division is into SIMPLE and COMPLEX. Simple perceptions or impressions and ideas are such that admit of no distinction or separation. The complex are the contrary to these, and may be distinguished into two parts. Tho' a particular colour, taste and smell are qualities all united together in this apple, 'tis easy to perceive they are not the same, but are at least distinguishable from each other. . . . *All our simple ideas in their first appearance are deriv'd from simple impressions, which are correspondent to them, and which they exactly represent.*

—*A Treatise of Human Nature*, Book 1

On cause and effect:

Thus not only our reason fails us in the discovery of the *ultimate connexion* of causes and effects, but even after experience has inform'd us of their *constant conjunction*, 'tis impossible for us to satisfy ourselves by our reason, why we shou'd extend that experience beyond those particular instances, which have fallen under our observation. We suppose, but we are never able to prove, that there must be a resemblance betwixt those objects, of which we have had experience, and those which lie beyond the reach of our discovery.

—*A Treatise of Human Nature*, Book 1

The impossibility of a continued and distinct existence:

We may well ask, *What causes induce us to believe in the existence of body?* but 'tis vain to ask, *Whether there be body or not?* That is a point, which we must take for granted in all our reasonings. . . . We ought to examine apart these two questions, which are commonly confounded together, *viz.* Why we attribute a CONTINU'D existence to objects, even when they are not present to the senses; and why we suppose them to have an existence DISTINCT from the mind. Under this last head I comprehend their situation as well as relations, their *external* position as well as the *independence* of their existence and operation. . . . [The senses] give us no notion of continued existence, because they cannot operate beyond the extent, in which they really operate. They as little produce the opinion of a distinct existence, because they neither can offer it to the mind as represented, nor as original. To offer it as represented, they must present both an object and an image. To make it appear as original, they must convey a falsehood; and this falsehood must lie in the relations and situation: In order to which they must be able to compare the object with ourselves; and even in that case they do not, nor is it possible they shou'd, deceive us. We may, therefore, conclude with certainty, that the opinion of a continu'd and a distinct existence never arises from the senses.

—*A Treatise of Human Nature*, Book 1

Whatever convincing arguments philosophers may fancy they can produce to establish the belief of objects independent of the mind, 'tis obvious these objects are known but to very few, and that 'tis not by them, that children, peasants, and the greater part of mankind are induc'd attribute objects to some impressions, and deny them to others. Accordingly we find, that all the conclusions, which the vulgar form on this head, are directly contrary to those, which are confirm'd by philosophy. For philosophy informs us, that every thing, which appears to the mind, is nothing but a perception, and is interrupted, and dependent on the mind; whereas the vulgar confound perceptions and objects, and attribute a distinct continu'd existence to the very things they feel or see. This sentiment, then, as it is entirely unreasonable, must proceed from some faculty other than the understanding. To which we may add, that as long as we take our perceptions and objects to be the same, we can never infer the existence of the one from that of the other, nor form any argument from the relation of cause and effect; which is the only one that can assure us of matter of fact. Even after we distinguish our perceptions from our objects, 'twill appear presently, that we are still incapable of reasoning from the existence of one to that of the other: So that upon the whole our reason neither does, nor is it possible it ever shou'd, upon any supposition, give us an assurance of the continu'd and distinct existence of body. That opinion must be entirely owing to the IMAGINATION.

—*A Treatise of Human Nature*, Book 1

Errors in religion are dangerous; those in philosophy only ridiculous.

—*A Treatise of Human Nature*, Book 2

Reason is, and ought only to be the slave of the passions, and can never pretend to any other office than to serve and obey them.

—*A Treatise of Human Nature*, Book 2

What philosophical truths can be more advantageous to society, than those here delivered, which represent virtue in all her genuine and most engaging charms, and makes us approach her with ease, familiarity, and affection? The dismal dress falls off, with which many divines, and some philosophers, have covered her; and nothing appears but gentleness, humanity, beneficence, affability; nay, even at proper intervals, play, frolic, and gaiety. She talks not of useless austerities and rigours, suffering and self-denial. She declares that her sole purpose is to make her votaries and all mankind, during every instant of their existence, if possible, cheerful and happy; nor does she ever willingly part with any pleasure but in hopes of ample compensation in some other period of their lives. The sole trouble which she demands, is that of just calculation, and a steady preference of the greater happiness. And if any austere pretenders approach her, enemies of joy and pleasure, she either rejects them as hypocrites and deceivers; or, if she admit them in her train, they are ranked, however, among the least favoured of her votaries.

—*An Enquiry Concerning the Principles of Morals*

I have often observed, that, among the French, the first questions with regard to a stranger are, *Is he polite? Has he wit?* In our own country, the chief praise bestowed is always that of a *good-natured, sensible fellow.*

—An Enquiry Concerning the Principles of Morals

Were the disposal of human life so much reserved as the peculiar province of the Almighty, that it were an encroachment on his life for men to dispose of their own lives, it would be equally criminal to act for the preservation of life as for its destruction. If I turn aside a stone which is falling upon my head, I disturb the course of nature; and I invade the peculiar province of the Almighty, by lengthening out my life beyond the period, which, by the general laws of matter and motion, he has assigned it.

A hair, a fly, an insect, is able to destroy this mighty being whose life is of such importance. Is it an absurdity to suppose that human prudence may lawfully dispose of what depends on such insignificant causes?

It would be no crime in me to divert the *Nile* or *Danube* from its course, were I able to effect such purposes. Where then is the crime of turning a few ounces of blood from their natural channels!

—"On Suicide"

The powers of men are no more superior to their wants, considered merely in this life, than those of foxes and hares are, compared to *their* wants and to *their* period of existence.

—"On the Immortality of the Soul"

Our insensibility before the composition of the body seems to natural reason a proof of a like state after dissolution.

—"On the Immortality of the Soul"

In Newton this island may boast of having produced the greatest and rarest genius that ever rose for the ornament and instruction of the species. Cautious in admitting no principles but such as were founded on experiment, but resolute to adopt every such principle, however new or unusual; from modesty, ignorant of his superiority above the rest of mankind, and thence less careful to accommodate his reasonings to common apprehensions; more anxious to merit than acquire fame; he was, from these causes, long unknown to the world. But his reputation at last broke out with a lustre which scarcely any writer, during his own lifetime, had ever before attained. . . .

Most of the celebrated writers of this age remain monuments of genius perverted by indecency and bad taste; and none more than Dryden, both by reason of the greatness of his talents and the gross abuse which he made of them. His plays, excepting a few scenes, are utterly disfigured by vice or folly, or both; his translations appear too much the offspring of haste and hunger; even his fables are ill-chosen tales, conveyed in an incorrect though spirited versification. Yet, amid this great number of loose productions, the refuse of our language, there are found some small pieces—his Ode to St. Cecilia, the greater part of Absalom and Achitophel, and a few more—which discover so great genius, such richness of expression, such pomp and variety of numbers, that they leave us equally full of regret and indignation on account of the inferiority, or, rather, great absurdity, of his other writings.

—The History of England

Look round this universe. What an immense profusion of beings, animated and organised, sensible and active! You admire this prodigious variety and fecundity. But inspect a little more narrowly these living existences, the only beings worth regarding. How hostile and destructive to each other! How insufficient all of them for their own happiness! How contemptible or odious to the spectator! The whole represents nothing but the idea of a blind nature, impregnated by a great vivifying principle, and pouring forth from her lap, without discernment or parental care, her maimed and abortive children.

—Dialogues Concerning Natural Religion

Chronology of Significant Philosophical Dates

6th C B.C.	The beginning of Western philosophy with Thales of Miletus.
End of 6th C B.C.	Death of Pythagoras.
399 B.C.	Socrates sentenced to death in Athens.
c 387 B.C.	Plato founds the Academy in Athens, the first university.
335 B.C.	Aristotle founds the Lyceum in Athens, a rival school to the Academy.

324 A.D.	Emperor Constantine moves capital of Roman Empire to Byzantium.
400 A.D.	St. Augustine writes his *Confessions*. Philosophy absorbed into Christian theology.
410 A.D.	Sack of Rome by Visigoths heralds opening of Dark Ages.
529 A.D.	Closure of Academy in Athens by Emperor Justinian marks end of Hellenic thought.
Mid-13th C	Thomas Aquinas writes his commentaries on Aristotle. Era of Scholasticism.
1453	Fall of Byzantium to Turks, end of Byzantine Empire.
1492	Columbus reaches America. Renaissance in Florence and revival of interest in Greek learning.
1543	Copernicus publishes *On the Revolution of the Celestial Orbs*, proving mathematically that the earth revolves around the sun.

1633	Galileo forced by church to recant heliocentric theory of the universe.
1641	Descartes publishes his *Meditations*, the start of modern philosophy.
1677	Death of Spinoza allows publication of his *Ethics*.
1687	Newton publishes *Principia*, introducing concept of gravity.
1689	Locke publishes *Essay Concerning Human Understanding*. Start of empiricism.
1710	Berkeley publishes *Principles of Human Knowledge*, advancing empiricism to new extremes.
1716	Death of Leibniz.
1739–1740	Hume publishes *Treatise of Human Nature*, taking empiricism to its logical limits.
1781	Kant, awakened from his "dogmatic slumbers" by Hume, publishes *Critique of Pure Reason*.

Great era of German metaphysics begins.

1807   Hegel publishes *The Phenomenology of Mind*, high point of German metaphysics.

1818   Schopenhauer publishes *The World as Will and Representation*, introducing Indian philosophy into German metaphysics.

1889   Nietzsche, having declared "God is dead," succumbs to madness in Turin.

1921   Wittgenstein publishes *Tractatus Logico-Philosophicus*, claiming the "final solution" to the problems of philosophy.

1920s   Vienna Circle propounds Logical Positivism.

1927   Heidegger publishes *Being and Time*, heralding split between analytical and Continental philosophy.

1943   Sartre publishes *Being and Nothingness*, advancing

Heidegger's thought and instigating existentialism.

1953   Posthumous publication of Wittgenstein's *Philosophical Investigations*. High era of linguistic analysis.

Chronology of Hume's Life

1711	David Hume born in Edinburgh.
1723	Enters Edinburgh University at age twelve.
1729	Suffers serious mental breakdown.
1734	Retires to France to write his philosophical masterpiece.
1739–1740	Publishes his *Treatise of Human Nature*, which attracts little attention.
1745–1746	Acts as tutor to mad Marquess of Anandale.

1746	Hume takes part in General St. Clair's farcical invasion of France.
1748	Publishes first collection of his *Essays*.
1754–1762	Publishes successive volumes of *History of England*.
1758	Publishes *An Enquiry Concerning Human Understanding*, essentially a rewrite of Volumes I and II of the *Treatise*.
1763	Becomes secretary to British Embassy in Paris.
1766	Brings Rousseau to England.
1769	Returns to live in Edinburgh.
1776	Dies after prolonged illness.

Recommended Reading

David Hume, *Selected Essays*, ed. by Stephen Copley (Oxford University Press, 1993). Always readable, they remain for the most part surprisingly topical.

David Hume, *A Treatise of Human Nature*, ed. by Ernest C. Mossner (Penguin Classics, 1986). Hume's great philosophical work.

Ernest C. Mossner, *The Life of David Hume* (Oxford University Press, 1980). The definitive life of Hume, presenting the man in all his aspects. Highly readable, too.

David F. Norton, ed., *The Cambridge Companion to Hume* (Cambridge University Press, 1993). A wide range of essays on Hume's thought.

RECOMMENDED READING

David Pears, *Hume's System: An Examination of the First Book of His Treatise* (Oxford University Press, 1991). A good detailed exegesis of Hume's epistemology.

Index

A NOTE ON THE AUTHOR

Paul Strathern has lectured in philosophy and mathematics and now lives and writes in London. A Somerset Maugham prize winner, he is also the author of books on history and travel as well as five novels. His articles have appeared in a great many publications, including the *Observer* (London) and the *Irish Times*. His own degree in philosophy was earned at Trinity College, Dublin.